TWO MOTHERS
AND THEIR 60-YEAR
SECRET

Author: Ben D. Rogers, D.Th.

Paul says, For our gospel came not unto you in word only, but also in power, and in the Holy Ghost, and in much assurance. (1 Thess. 1:5) Why are so many pulpits today void of effective evangelical gospel preaching, preachers of power and much assurance? Is the Holy Spirit totally at fault here? We dare not think so. Has the Bible sermon, the Christian sermon, the evangelist sermon or the Gospel itself lost its power? Perish the thought. Rather, this book demonstrates that the lack of power is in the failure to effectively reach men. The purpose of this book is to be a clear guide for preachers today, using the Scriptures to create a basis for persuasive evangelistic preaching.

The subject of this book is limited to one type of sermon... the evangelistic sermon. Four basic appeals in evangelistic preaching are expounded and organized in useful format. Actual sermon outlines, structure and delivery of the sermon will be much more obvious after the very foundation of an effective sermon is dealt with as spelled out in this book.

One of the primary needs in the effort of evangelistic preaching is to establish the relative place of the mind, the conscience, the emotions and the will in one's appeal. Many criticize proclamation evangelism as securing decisions by appeals largely emotional and generally void of any intellectual involvement. It is therefore necessary to establish the truth that true evangelistic preaching involves each of the elements of man's soul and not just his emotions. Through effective evangelism, the Holy Spirit touches each aspect of man's makeup and enables his decision for salvation, as is expounded in the gospel of Jesus Christ.

TWO MOTHERS
AND THEIR 60-YEAR
SECRET

Opening the Doors
to a Private Adoption

Nita B. Rogers

LIFE SENTENCE
Publishing, LLC

www.lifesentencepublishing.com

Like us on Facebook

Two Mothers and Their Sixty-Year Secret – Nita B. Rogers

Copyright © 2014

Printed in the United States of America

First edition published 2013

LIFE SENTENCE Publishing books are available at discounted prices for ministries and other outreach. Find out more by contacting us at info@lifesentencepublishing.com

LIFE SENTENCE Publishing and its logo are trademarks of

LIFE SENTENCE Publishing, LLC
P.O. Box 652
Abbotsford, WI 54405

Paperback ISBN: 978-1-62245-146-3

Ebook ISBN: 978-1-62245-147-0

10 9 8 7 6 5 4 3 2 1

This book is available from www.amazon.com, Barnes & Noble, and your local Christian bookstore.

Cover Design: Amber Burger

Editor: Sheila Wilkinson

Share this book on Facebook

Dedication

I want to dedicate this book to all the teenage or adult women who, faced with a crisis pregnancy, have made the decision to choose life and give the innocent unborn an opportunity to live and make contributions to others in this world. Only God knows all the potential of each new life. It is my hope that this book will remind you that giving life is the most loving act you can do for yourself and all involved.

I would also like to dedicate this work to those adopted people who may now be attempting to search out their biological heritage. It is hard not to become obsessed with facts you find and the difficulties you encounter along the way. Remember, God is in control of every part of our lives. He has given you one life to live. Make it count for God and for the good of others.

Finally, I dedicate this story to my best friend, my lifelong love, my husband, Ben, who has always told people that "Nita is the best argument against abortion that I know." He has been with me from the beginning of my search, dealing with my emotions, keeping me balanced, and reminding me that God has watched over every step of my life and will use my story to His glory.

It is my prayer that God will use this story to warm hearts, give encouragement, and glorify my Lord and Savior, Jesus Christ.

– Nita B. Rogers, Longview, Texas, November 2013

Contents

Acknowledgements

I gratefully acknowledge with thanks the following special people:

Karen Bozeman, English and Journalism teacher, long-time friend and supporter, who gently pointed me to the very best way to tell the story.

Dr. Sandee Williams, who kept me focused on the amazing work God has done.

Ruth, Ben Jr., Becky, and Anna, who lovingly read the story and had a great part in it.

The staff of Life Sentence Publishing who has used their professional and creative abilities to produce this work.

Foreword

I have traveled all over the world with Nita Rogers. What I know of her from those travels is that she is a kind and faithful friend with a terrific sense of humor, a dedicated mother, and a loving wife. Nita is also a woman of prayer and committed to the ministry of the Lord.

Sometime later, I learned that she was searching for her birth parents. It was clear to me that Nita knew who she was and whose she was. This quest was not about "finding herself," rather, it was the pursuit of God's path in her life. Nita has always been aware that her adoption was for reasons that only He knew but would reveal to her later in life.

In the Bible, there are lengthy passages designed to demonstrate who begot whom. So it makes sense that adopted children have an intense desire to know who begot them. I had seen this type of exploration before by adopted adult children – some having good results and some with poor results. However, there was something different about this particular journey. In this search, the Lord had important things in mind that would result from Nita's mission to discover who begot her.

– Dr. Sandee Williams

CHAPTER ONE

The Oath

*K*eeping a secret is a challenge to all people, men and women alike. But I have always heard that women just don't know how to keep a secret. The old saying goes, "Telephone, telegraph or tell a woman." In my life there were two women who promised each other they would never share their personal secret. They never did! Only after years of searching did I come to understand just how their lives had crossed. I still do not understand why they felt so strongly about keeping their oath to each other.

The first woman was in her early twenties, unmarried and seeking help to deal with a crisis pregnancy. The second one was nearing forty years of age with no prospect of having children unless she and her husband were given a baby. Their paths crossed for a moment in time when they agreed to an adoption that would be handled in the most private condition possible.

When one passed a newborn to the other, their promise was sealed in their hearts. These two mothers never spoke of their connection to one another and never talked to anyone about one another. Whether they handled the adoption of that baby in the best way or not, they stayed true to each other. They decided that once the transaction was made, they would never discuss it again.

Did either of them realize the amazing plan God was setting in motion? Maybe not, but there was a plan that called for a step of faith from each of them.

I realize now that my life was touched by these two mothers. I have come to know them both, to appreciate each one's place in my life, and to accept their individuality. Now that I have experienced the funerals of both of these mothers, I know how the awesome hand of God kept us apart for my sixty-year journey to the truth. Yet in due time, God brought us together.

When I was a child, my parents never talked with me about adoption. My childhood friends broke the news to me. Somehow I never considered it necessary to find out about my biological parents until after my adoptive mother died in 1989. As my own family grew and I looked for physical resemblances and traits, my desire to look backward into my roots grew. When each grandchild was born, someone would say they looked like folks in my husband's families. Surely there were characteristics from my own ancestors, I thought. So when I began to ask questions in my extended family, some of them roused my interest by reporting several things they had heard.

I loved, honored, and appreciated the wonderful parents that I had. My mother was committed to raising her little girl with every fiber of her being. She loved me, disciplined me, and tried to prepare me for life as she thought best. We were close throughout her life, sharing much time together when my daddy was away. Mother was a good listener, full of fun, and a people-lover, yet she had a sharp tongue that caused some problems. Mother was living in my home when she died, and her death was a great personal loss. She was the only mother I knew. I have often called her "the president of my fan club" because she was a great encourager.

Little did I imagine that I would locate the mother who gave me life and then gave me to a family that would love and care for me. Her heartbreak and sacrifice as a young woman must have been heavy on her heart. She said she never told her family or her husband. Finding her brought new emotions and new facts about my biological heritage. It was an unbelievable experience to also attend a funeral for this precious woman many years later. My life is truly a story of two mothers – both of whom were irreplaceable in my life. Amazingly, both of them kept their oral pact and did not talk to anyone else or to me!

Several outcomes of my search totally surprised me while others left me amazed at the two women who came together so briefly. Every decision we make affects not only the future of our own lives but the lives of others. In relation to adoption, this is abundantly true.

When I began this journey, I quickly realized that this effort could develop into something obsessive, disappointing, or distressing. Every adopted child should be motivated by an "attitude of gratitude" initially because he or she has had a home and received love and care. Any attempt to find biological parents for selfish or vengeful reasons will only add confusion and disappointment to the situation.

My search has left some unanswered questions. However, my findings have left me more convinced than ever that God is in control of all things. I have believed this all my life – what I discovered only confirms that truth. God's mercy, grace, and abounding love have followed me from one disclosure to another. It has been like opening one door only to see another door just ahead. Every door requires a decision – to enter or not.

With that, I share my journey through the doors of my private adoption.

CHAPTER TWO

The Early Years

For a little girl growing up in the Cedar Grove section of Shreveport, Louisiana, in the 1940s, life was wonderful. My father, Tommie B. Brock, worked in the oil fields of north Louisiana and Texas, so my mother and I would pack up and move with him to a town near the location where the well was being drilled. We rented an apartment, started attending a good church, and made friends from the town as well as among the folks Daddy worked with.

My earliest memories were of packing dishes, bed linens, clothes, and household goods into the back seat of a Ford sedan. (Daddy always drove a Ford to work.) There was room on top of all these boxes and piles of household goods for me to crawl on for a nap or to color as we traveled. When I wasn't riding in the back seat, I rode on a wooden crate in the middle of the front seat between Mother and Daddy. It was great fun riding up high enough to see out the windshield. When Daddy stopped to get gas at a filling station, he would come back to the car with icy-cold Grapettes to drink as we continued the trip. "Watch this bump. That bottle may crack a tooth if it hits," was my Mother's warning. I never cracked a tooth, but I did try to watch ahead for holes and dips in the road. Of course, there were no four-lane interstates.

One place I vividly recall was Bay City, Texas. We lived for a time in a garage apartment. I remember Daddy moved us into the downtown hotel during a hurricane threat in South Texas. We had a room on the third floor. The wind blew so hard against the window that rain poured in over the windowsill, and the carpet was drenched. Mother and I went down to the lobby where I had a great time playing with my dolls among the greenery in the sitting area of the lobby. The hotel was full of people who had escaped from their homes.

Later we moved into a duplex next door to a couple who had no children – Sgt. and Mrs. Crawford. Mrs. Crawford was crippled from arthritis, but she was a great neighbor. It was at this home that I celebrated my fifth birthday with a party. The Bay City newspaper carried an article about little "Miss Nita Brock" who had a grand time with friends and family.

Being an only child, sometimes I got lonesome. What would a little girl do to combat such feelings? Well, I had an imaginary puppy. Somewhere I found a dog leash, and I dragged it behind me, talking to my puppy and enjoying its company. Our neighbor once heard me go by her window talking to my dog. She asked my Mother when Nita got a dog. "She doesn't have a dog!" Mother answered. Very shortly my temporary, invisible friend disappeared.

In 1941, we were living in Bay City when World War II began. Daddy came home one day driving a brand new Pontiac sedan. It was the last new car received by the dealership before the United States entered the war. We were really proud that it had been delivered before times changed for all Americans.

I was enrolled in Miss Tenie Holmes' private kindergarten in Bay City. Mother felt that I needed to learn to play with other children and make friends. I wore my cowboy boots to school with my ruffled dresses. Pictures verify my style! In addition to teaching us how to write and beginner's reading, Miss Tenie taught us manners. She would set a chair at the front of the class and have each student say, "Excuse me," as we walked in front of her. We had a choice every morning of ordering the most wonderful chocolate milk or ice-cold orange drink for our snack time.

I successfully "graduated" from kindergarten in Bay City. We moved back to Shreveport where Daddy had built a nice two-bedroom, one-bath house at 6403 Henderson Avenue. It was built in about 1932. Daddy paid a Mr. Elder, who was the builder, $3,200 for it – "cash on the barrelhead" as Daddy would say. The house at 6403 was about half a block from Southside Baptist Church. Mother and Daddy were already members, and Mother had been very active in a Sunday school class, Women's Missionary Union (WMU), and the choir when we were in town while Daddy worked away.

The women at Southside Baptist had given Mother a baby shower when I was "born." Naturally they all knew that Mother had not given birth to a baby, but Mother always spoke of my birth as if she had done it herself even though she was thirty-eight years old. Some said she even went to bed to show that she had had a baby. This type of denial was maintained by Mother for years among her friends. I always felt that they knew something about me that they weren't telling. Everyone knew I was adopted – except me!

It was told among the family that Mother had kept baby clothes in the house for two years prior to my birth, hoping that someone would have a baby for her. I am not sure how she expected to receive a baby unless the family doctor, Dr. George G. Garrett, was watching out for a baby who needed a home with my folks in mind. Mother and Daddy were in their late thirties, but God answered their prayers. He sent a baby to them in His perfect time.

CHAPTER THREE

School Years

After settling in Shreveport in 1942, I was enrolled in Fairfield Elementary School. Because I had been to kindergarten, Mr. Beckham, the principal, and Mrs. Stone, the second grade teacher, agreed that I might be able to go on to the second grade, skipping the first. School was a challenge because there were so many kids I didn't know surrounding me. Every time we went outside for recess, I walked home. When I got home, Mother would patiently walk me back to school. I did adapt, but only after the school officials threatened to put me back in the first grade.

During a walk home with my playmates from across the street, the Carey twins, something was said about my mother and daddy. One of them said, "They aren't really your mother and daddy."

My childlike anger flared, and I replied, "Yes, they are my mother and daddy!"

"Go ask them," was the challenge from these girls.

That was exactly what I did. I ran home, pushed open the screen door, and went into the house to ask. Mother was taking a bath, and I called to her through the bathroom door, "Mother, they said I am not your little girl!"

I have never forgotten Mother's calm reply, "Yes, you are our little girl, and you will always be our little girl."

To my remembrance, that was the last time in my childhood years that anything was ever said about my adoption. The word adoption was not used. For some reason, my heart was satisfied, and I never asked any more questions. The secret mother had promised to keep was still very safe in her heart.

Year by year, I progressed through grade school. Grades one through three had classrooms on the first floor, but in the fourth grade, we moved to second-floor classrooms. That was a great day. My fourth grade teacher was the wife of the man who invented Ipana toothpaste. She was very conscientious about health and hygiene. Every day we went through the routine of checking fingernails, ears, and teeth. She also taught the girls in the class to walk with several books on our heads to improve our posture. That was the year I discovered long division – math became my enemy at school. I thought I never would understand division. Decades later I would marvel that two of our daughters were teaching math.

Following seventh grade, all the Fairfield students went to Byrd High School. There was no junior high for us. My class was the last one to spend five years in high school because a new junior high in Shreveport opened the next year. Going to Byrd opened up another world for me. I met friends from all over the east side of Shreveport. I became involved in school activities with the History Club, Library Club, Future Homemakers, choir, and a girls' social club. I had been taking piano lessons since the age of six. During my junior and senior years at Byrd, I took private voice lessons and began to sing at school, as well as in the Shreveport Civic Chorus, but primarily in the church youth choir.

All this information about my childhood is important to my story because as I have discovered, I lived around people who might have known both my biological parents. They, too, lived in Shreveport, and some were quite well known in business and political circles. However, during those years I was happy, secure, successful as a student, and growing as a Christian. I never wondered about my background, never asked questions of my parents, and was moving through life with absolutely no insecurity. None of my friends ever teased me about being adopted or treated me like there was any difference among us. I was loved, accepted, and affirmed by peers and teachers.

In 1953, I was a senior at Byrd High School. It was a wonderful, successful time as I enjoyed my friends, my classes, and my activities at school. I was president of the Library Club and the History Club and was inducted into the National Honor Society. I finished my voice lessons by giving a voice recital at the Louisiana Fairgrounds Auditorium, singing in English, Latin, French and German for the first and last times. Daddy had surprised Mother and me by buying a 1953 Buick Super which was mine to drive back and forth to school. I was at the top. At the honors assembly before graduation, I was presented the Woodman of the World Award for History. Byrd graduates did not wear the traditional caps and gowns for graduation, but the girls wore formal white dresses and carried bouquets of red roses. I don't know how all the students were able to afford this luxurious attire, but it made graduation exercises exciting.

Prior to graduation in the spring, I began to search for the college I wanted to attend. Several schools were presented to me at different functions. I wanted to go to a Christian college, but wasn't sure where that should be. My parents were not financially able to provide a lot of luxuries, but they were committed to my education. Early in my life, they took out a thousand dollar policy for my college expenses. As unbelievable as it seems, that amount paid for my entire freshman year – tuition, room and board, books, etc. I considered Blue Mountain College in Alabama which was an all-girls school at that time. But several of my friends from Southside Baptist had gone to Baylor University in Waco, Texas. I spent a weekend there and decided that was the right place for me. I was excited about leaving home, doing my own thing, and getting on with my life.

Every advantage, success, and opportunity that came to me during these years affirmed the purpose God had for my future. He was just beginning to unfold His plan.

CHAPTER FOUR

My Christian Growth

$\mathscr{S}$hortly after my grade school encounter about my adoption, I became interested in becoming a Christian. I had been in Sunday school and mission organizations (Sunbeams and Girls Auxiliary) with godly women who were concerned about each child they taught. Our church was also blessed with a wonderful, seventh-grade, public school teacher, Mrs. Ruby Keith, who made it her mission to witness to each child in our church during services. She would make her way down the row and say to each of us, "Do you need to trust Jesus?" One morning when she spoke to me, my heart responded because I knew I did need Jesus as Savior.

Some time later on a Sunday morning when my mother and daddy were not in church, I walked forward during the invitation hymn and told our pastor, Rev. J. F. Kane, that I wanted to trust Jesus. No one counseled me, but I have never doubted that the decision I made that morning changed my life. My Grandmother Brock was the only member of my family in the service that day. She came by in the welcome line, hugged me, and shared the day with me. After the service, I went out the back door of the church, jumped the drainage ditch along the street, and ran home. It seemed that the sky was bluer, the grass was greener, and absolute joy filled my eight-year-old heart. I went in the front door and told Daddy who was reading the comics and Mother who was cooking lunch that I had asked Jesus to come into my heart. They shared my joy.

Following my decision to be saved, I realized that I would need to take a step of obedience and be baptized. With an absolute fear of going under water, I stepped into the baptistry the next Sunday along with several friends who had also made salvation decisions. When my foot touched the warm water, my fear was gone. It was the right thing to do, and God took all fear away.

I am convinced that the decision I made that Sunday morning was not only spiritually life-changing, but gave me an anchor for life in the love and direction of God as well as a family of Christian brothers and sisters that still give me identity as a child of God. I was never shaken by the facts of my life that I did not know then and do not know now. If God loves me and has a plan for my life just like I am, there is no need for me to question my biological heritage. I know God predestined the family I have on earth as well as in heaven.

I became more active in the church as I grew older. I was involved in Bible Memory Association and memorized the most wonderful passages of Scripture. My time in Girls' Auxiliary taught me about missions, missionaries, community missions with hospitals, the sick, and the needy of our city. Each spring we were recognized for our accomplishments as we moved through the various steps of this group. I convinced my parents to allow me to go to the Louisiana Youth Camp held each summer for ten days at Mandeville Encampment on the shores of Lake Ponchartrain. A caravan of buses would leave Shreveport and travel down the state, picking up other buses as we went. Again the Lord gave me some wonderful, lifelong friends during these experiences. We heard good Bible preachers, missionaries, and wonderful Bible study leaders.

In 1951, a young man came to our church as youth director. Little did we realize what a lasting influence he would have in the lives of about fifty of us. Quinn Pugh was a student at East Texas Baptist College in Marshall, Texas, who drove to Shreveport to spend days and weekends building a youth program and a youth choir. He was among the first people to hold a ministry position just for youth in the Southern Baptist Convention. He was a trained, talented singer and began to teach us all kinds of wonderful music – from "My God Is Real" to Handel's "Messiah" and Dubois' "Seven Last Words." We even sang Fred Waring's arrangement of "Battle Hymn of the Republic." We traveled to churches in the summer to sing choir concerts and spent a week each summer at Daingerfield Encampment to learn conducting as well as music for special concerts.

Among the members of the youth group was a young man who became a good friend of mine. In 1952 during a youth revival, he had surrendered to the gospel ministry at the age of sixteen. The same night as a fourteen-year-old, I made a commitment of my life to do whatever God wanted me to do. As it happened, we knelt on opposite ends of the same pew. I recall sharing my decision with my mother and daddy. All Daddy was able to say was, "I want you to do what God wants, but just don't go to Africa to be a missionary." I didn't – until I was 67 years old. After retiring, I joined my husband in four trips to Malawi, east Africa, doing village evangelism and church planting.

The young man who was my friend back then was Ben Rogers. We spent hours talking together before church in the church library. He told me his problems and dreams, and I shared mine. I had selected as a life verse Matthew 6:33: *But seek first the kingdom of God and His righteousness, and all these things shall be added to you.* Little did I know just how many things God would add to my life as I followed Him.

Ben graduated from Byrd High School a year before me and went on to Louisiana College, Pineville, Louisiana, in the summer of 1952. He began serving churches during revivals as music director. He became the summer youth director at Caddo Heights Baptist Church in Shreveport. He soon was preaching his own youth revivals and became widely used after he got to college. He was my friend, and I was happy that God was using him. I watched him lead his youth choir and preach on Sunday nights the summer before I left for Baylor. It seemed our paths were going in different directions. Both of us were totally committed to doing God's will for our lives. Little did we know what He had in store.

CHAPTER FIVE

Getting Married

*I*n high school, I dated some and spent a couple of years
going steady with a young man in the church youth
group. But when I became a high school senior, he had already
gone on to college, and I wanted to break up that relationship
so I could have more freedom to date. Actually, I did not like
the way he assumed that I would always be available when he
was at home from college. So when I left home for Baylor, I did
the unthinkable – I wrote him a "Dear John" letter telling him
I did not want to date him or see him again. It was not the right
way to do that, but it was the only way I knew I could just stop
seeing him. It worked. He tried to get Mother to speak up for
him, but she would not.

I met several fine young men at Baylor and was dating
one when I came home for the Thanksgiving holiday. After
a youth fellowship at Southside, I met Ben and he walked me
home – half a block down the street from the church. When
we got to my house, he said maybe we could make a date for
the Christmas holidays. He promised to write me, and I was
excited that he might really be interested in me. We did write

between Thanksgiving and the Christmas holidays. We made a date to see the Christmas lights in downtown Shreveport on December 21. In the meantime, the young man I was dating at Baylor got very serious about us during the Christmas holiday – without my knowledge. He felt that God's will was for us to marry. That scared me to death. He had spoken to his pastor and was fully convinced we were meant to be. I certainly did not share that idea. When I got home for the holidays, he sent a dozen red roses which were very noticeable when Ben came to pick me up for our first date. Needless to say, we talked about the roses and the fellow who sent them.

We were already friends, so the beginning of a dating relationship led quickly to the fact that we were in love. I went back to Baylor, broke off the relationship with the other fellow, and began writing and phoning Louisiana College several times a week. We prayed separately about what God wanted for us. We both traveled to Shreveport to spend time together. Ben was preaching a lot on Sundays, so we would be together on Friday night or Saturday, and then he would be off to a church somewhere in Louisiana to preach. It was a five-hour bus ride from Waco to Shreveport, but Ben was always there to meet the bus in downtown Shreveport, and we would enjoy time together. I completed my first year of college at Baylor and came home for the summer.

In the fall of 1954, I transferred to Louisiana College. Ben and I began to ask God to make a way for us to get married. We felt that he needed to have a full-time pastorate in order to have an income, so as soon as a church extended an invitation for him to be pastor, we made plans for a wedding. My parents were living in Tallulah, Louisiana, where Daddy was drilling a well. We drove up there one Friday night so Ben could ask them for my hand in marriage. What a custom! Mother had a supper of her famous fried chicken and all the trimmings. I kept waiting for Ben to bring up the subject of marriage. Neither of us could eat a bite, and I finally took my fork and pressed it into Ben's thigh to get him to say something! He and Daddy went to the front porch and sat down in a porch swing. The higher they went, the faster Ben talked, and finally Daddy gave his blessing – just to get out of the swing, I suspect!

That same night we set the date for December 21, 1954 – one year from our first official date. With their approval, we drove back to the campus. Mother had packed the fried chicken we could not eat during the meal. The highway from Tallulah to Pineville was littered with chicken bones as we made up for the supper we weren't able to eat. There were no litterbug laws in those days.

At this point, Mother called Ben in for a talk without my knowledge or presence. She related to Ben that I was adopted, and he did not have to be afraid to marry me because I was from one of the finest families in Louisiana. It was her way of assuring him that there was no mental illness or such in my history, I guess. After they talked, Ben shared with me what she had said. It angered me that it was done behind my back, but I never said anything to Mother about it. I'm not sure why, unless I felt that her secrecy made it clear that I was not to discuss it. I was so sure that it was God's will for us to be married that I just put it behind me, and plans went on. Once again Mother kept her secret, only sharing what she felt was necessary.

Ben was ordained on November 28, 1954, at Southside Baptist Church. We were married on December 21, 1954, and we began our life together as pastor and wife on the Sunday after Christmas in Alexandria, Louisiana. The effect of my adoption on our ministry was of little concern. God's patience and grace followed me every step of the way.

CHAPTER SIX

Raising a Family

My adoption was the furthest thing from my mind for many years. I was focused on being a good wife, pastor's wife, and soon a mother. During the next seven years our family boomed – a girl, a boy, and then three more girls. Our third child was born when the first two were still toddlers. She came into this world with more challenges than any of us imagined possible. She was not only hydrocephalic, but had spina bifida that left her with no control in her lower body. Doctors were kind about her condition, but felt she would only live a week or so. Only two major hospitals in the United States were experimenting with shunts to relieve the pressure of spinal fluids. As a young pastor's family, we were not financially able to travel to either place or pay for the treatment necessary.

Expecting her life to be cut short, the hospital administrators allowed her to stay in the hospital nursery for their special attention and care. Every day her little body was getting weaker. We prepared to care for her even though we had little hope. Mollie Christine lived for four-and-a-half months before God Himself ended the struggle we all had endured. I felt our family was complete with a daughter, Ruth, and a son, Ben Jr. Two years later Rebecca was born, and a year later Anna was added to the family. God had taken one little girl and replenished our family with two more.

I began to understand what it was like to give up a child, although I believed that Mollie was safely at home in heaven and I would see her again.

In 1964, Ben became pastor of a church in St. Louis, Missouri. We had pastored churches in the Shreveport area for ten years. There I had the support of our parents and Ben's sister. We were able to have Sunday lunch with grandparents, Christmas events with both Ben's folks and my mother, who had been widowed. When one of the children was sick, I had phone calls and offers to help every morning to be sure I was taking good care of the grandchildren. But when we took the four grandchildren away from Shreveport to the metropolitan area of St. Louis, none of us was sure that I was up to the task of raising these children on my own.

We moved to St. Louis into a comfortable parsonage during the Thanksgiving weekend. For the next six weeks, we drove to church in snow and on icy streets. During the winter, we faced sore throats, fevers, earaches, and flu. When the weather finally became spring-like, I realized that all six of us had survived. I audibly said to myself, "We have all lived through this winter even without two grandmothers, a grandfather, and an aunt to check on us." Nothing since then has been a bigger boost to my ego.

I look back to the years when all our family grew together. I had never had any experience with children, so my days as a mother were truly my education. My interests up to then had been singing and playing the piano but not homemaking. I learned far more from my little children than they learned from me. Ben was patient with me, knowing I was doing the best I knew to do. I had to learn to cook, take care of babies, and be his wife. I learned to make gravy so the meal would go further, and in desperation I learned to sew. With three little girls and limited funds, I realized that sewing would provide some clothes for all of us. Thank God for the grandmothers who did all of that when I couldn't.

Those days went by in a blur. Ruth went to school before Becky was born. Ben Jr. started the year Anna was born. And days flew by until all were in school. They kept us busy, happy, and tired. I say the happiest days of my life were when they were all at home under my feet. Vacations, birthdays, family visits, friends from school and church, graduations, college students, plus all the church and school activities made time fly. The girls started piano lessons; Ben Jr. played baseball and later varsity tennis. All the children learned to drive with few incidents. We were blessed with puppies, a calico cat who had five kittens at the end of Ben Jr.'s bed, a chicken from a school incubator project, turtles, a couple of ill-fated hamsters, and one white rat.

In 1972, before Ruth and Ben had graduated from high school, Ben resigned from his pastorate at Hazelwood Baptist Church and entered full-time evangelism. Together we formed his nonprofit association and launched into his ministry of evangelism. It was truly a life lived by faith with no guaranteed income from week to week. Up to this point, I had been a stay-at-home mom. I was blessed to find a great place to enter the work force. I was employed by the Billy Graham St. Louis Crusade to open the crusade office and schedule events leading to the St. Louis Crusade in November of 1973. In the following years, I served as a church secretary and also as secretary-treasurer of Ben Rogers Evangelistic Association. I took some college courses, so I could work as a substitute teacher in the St Louis area. God was so good to provide every need we had. Ben's overseas mission crusades increased, and he served scores of churches in Missouri and many other states.

Having a husband and father away from home for weeks at a time caused me and the children to depend on each other and the Lord Jesus for so many things. Income varied from week to week. Keeping the financial books and paying bills was another challenge for me. I looked at the future and knew only God could supply our needs. At the conclusion of Ben's first full year in "faith" evangelism, I looked back and saw the hand of God meeting our needs at every turn. My trust in God began to grow stronger as I watched Him care for us.

Ruth was accepted at East Texas Baptist College, Marshall, Texas, only a few miles from the grandparents in Shreveport, so she began college. Ben Jr. had a job in the area at a discount department store. Becky and Anna were finishing grade school and going into junior high. They would come home from school, call me to check in, and get suggestions for supper. Both of them learned to cook as a help to their working mother. Ben was away from home often, and on Sunday evenings, Ben Jr. became the family chef, concocting all manner of interesting soups, sandwiches, and always ice cream. The next year Ben Jr. also began college at East Texas Baptist.

In 1976, we had two children in college in Marshall, Texas, so we pulled up our Missouri roots and moved to Longview, Texas. We were again near our mothers who were both widows by that time. I also went to work at LeTourneau University in the Financial Aid Office where I learned to back up files on a giant computer. The contacts with students from around the world made each day special.

Our lives were exciting with never a dull moment. We had four teenagers for a year and later four college students for a year. And then in 1977, we had two weddings. Our family was growing again. Without doubt, God was blessing my life, but the haunting truth of my adoption now came to my mind regularly. I thought, perhaps, it was time I brought up the subject with Mother.

CHAPTER SEVEN

Widening My Search

*I*n 1978, Mother's health was fragile, so before too much time had passed, she came to live with us. We made room for her, handled her doctors, finances and daily needs. I tried several times to approach her about the circumstances of my adoption. Once she told me that she was so determined to have a baby that she told Daddy she would take a black baby. That was quite a statement since my daddy would have died on the spot if that had happened. She also told me that she spoke to my biological mother once and pled with her to let them have her baby when it was born. But those were the only things Mother would share, and she was so defensive and uncomfortable talking about it that I just dropped the subject. She never said where or how she had met the birth mother. So the secret between these two mothers was kept almost two more decades.

Mother passed away in December 1987 at the age of 89 while she was living with us in Jacksonville, Florida. We had bought a home there. Ben was Associate Professor at Luther Rice Seminary and continued evangelistic meetings around the country as well as his overseas crusades. Again I found a fulfilling job in the Department of Evangelism of the Florida Baptist State Convention that was a perfect fit for my interests. I also completed my college degree after thirty-eight years. As I stood before the graduation banquet crowd to sing, I felt Mother would have been pleased to know that I finally had a degree.

Cautiously, I began to ask questions in the family – nieces and cousins – about what they knew about my adoption. From 1989 until 1993, I made several attempts to find information from vital birth records, marriage records, even writing to the Bureau of Vital Statistics in Baton Rouge, Louisiana. I contacted Schumpert Hospital in Shreveport, but they stated they did not give out information of that kind. Once I called the wife of Dr. Garrett, who seemed upset by a request for information and refused to even discuss her husband's role in my birth, even though she had worked as his nurse. I met dead ends at every turn.

Another interesting turn of events happened when Ben's mother was working at Schumpert Hospital and had an encounter with Dr. Garrett. They walked toward the elevator, and she mentioned my name to him. Standing at the elevator door, he said, "You know who her father is, don't you?" And in a flash, he stepped into the elevator, and the door closed. It just wasn't meant to be at that time. Still a father's name has never been told.

In late May of 1992, I wrote to two of Mother's nieces asking if either of them had any information that Mother might have given them related to my adoption. I received a beautiful letter from Mother's foster sister saying that nothing was ever told to her. She was thirteen when she overheard that, "Aunt Minnie had a baby." She said she knew Aunt Minnie had not been pregnant, but at that time, thirteen-year-olds didn't ask questions, so she never asked about it.

Ben and I made a trip to Korea and Japan for Luther Rice Seminary in June of 1992. When we returned, I had a message on my answering machine from one of the nieces. She said she had information about the matter I wrote about, but she did not want to put her information in a letter. She said I could call her if I wanted the information from her. I waited two days, praying and deciding whether to call her back. However, I concluded they might have some information since they were teenagers when I came into the family and could have heard talk.

When I called her, she told me she had heard that my biological mother was the daughter of a judge or attorney in the Baton Rouge area, but was originally from North Louisiana. That was not much to go on. She had no names and was not even certain about locations or situations.

Another niece told me that after my adoption, my birth mother came to see me at home on Henderson Street in Shreveport. She later asked to come again, but was refused. Mother and Daddy offered her money, but she refused, saying that she was satisfied knowing that her baby was in a Christian home. Mother never said anything to me about this visit.

I did remember once when I had gone in for supper, my friends told me that a car with a lady and two men had stopped in the street and asked them if Nita Brock lived at that house. My cousin also remembered being at Mother's when the same car passed the house six times. Whether those stories had any connection to my biological parents, I have never found out.

These family members also said that both Mother and Daddy

denied the actual adoption to friends and co-workers. I know that Mother always talked about "having me" and even told others that she had experienced labor. The ladies at Southside Baptist gave her a baby shower. These cards are in Mother's records to this day. I am sure they all knew the circumstances, even though Mother played a different game. Once a co-worker said, "Tommie's gone and adopted him a baby."

Daddy replied, "Hell, no, I didn't adopt no baby!" That sounds just like my Daddy's attitude. They were very proud and kept up their denial of the facts. All these instances point out that they intended to keep the secret.

Later in 1992, the phone rang and it was Winfred, Mother's great niece and the closest cousin to me. We had played together as children, and she was one of my wedding attendants. Word had gotten around in the family that I was asking about my adoption. For an hour, we talked about what neither of us was sure of. The conclusion of her call was that she believed we are really blood kin. She believed that her uncle might have been the father. She based this on the fact that Ben Jr. and her nephew looked alike in baby pictures taken of both of them at the same age.

I felt it was unlikely that the nieces would not have known this fact since their brother and his wife had died, and there would be no reason not to tell it if it was known to the family. She said she hoped that would not be a problem for me. I assured Winfred that it would make no difference to me who my birth parents were since I had only known one family during my life. I also told her that if I found out any information that I felt she and her relatives needed to know, I would get back in touch with her.

If I had been the child of her nephew, I believe Mother would have protected me from all of that part of the family to keep them from taking me from her. They never had any special connection to me, but watched as I cared for "Aunt Minnie" as she got older. I certainly never saw any family resemblances. I'm not sure how they thought their brother (uncle) would have been linked to the daughter of an attorney and/or judge in Baton Rouge when he was about twenty years old or why the young woman would have come to northwest Louisiana to live while she was pregnant if the father of her child also lived in that area. These were far-fetched ideas to me. The information these family members gave me never satisfied me. I always felt that the aunts, uncles, and cousins on both sides of the family were not quite sure how to handle the matter.

My daddy's brothers were wonderful and very attentive, even spoiling me, I think. Both my grandmothers were alive when I was a child. Mother's mother, Mama Cassel, was a fun-loving woman who was a great cook. Grandmother Brock was a rather somber woman, a good Bible teacher, and the mother of three sons. Both grandmothers were loving toward me. Mother and Daddy had been close to their nieces and nephews before I was born. All the Brock brothers lived on Henderson Street when I came into the family.

At birth, I was given an interesting name by Mother and Daddy. Daddy was working for Greer-Robinson Oil Company in 1936. Mr. Greer's wife's name was Nita. His secretary was a Miss Camille Mulholland. Thus the name Nita Camille was given to me.

As I grew older, Mother would take me by the Greer's home on Trabue in Shreveport for a short visit. It was almost like an appearance for her information and approval. Then at holidays, we would make a visit to Miss Camille's home on Margaret Place in Shreveport. It seemed that Mother wanted both of them to know that I was doing well and developing into a nice young lady. Even after our children were born, they were taken by Miss Camille's for a brief visit. Their interest in my welfare has been a very intriguing part of my story, but Mother never gave any explanation for these visits.

Another twist of events occurred years later. According to Mother, she and Daddy picked me up at Schumpert Hospital when I was three days old. Daddy died in 1955. When Daddy's will was probated, Mother and I sat down to read the document. There I saw that Tommie Brock's surviving family included his widow and his daughter, Nita Camille Brock Rogers, adopted on April 7, 1959. "Mother! How could this be?" She told me that when they signed the adoption papers in 1936, the document was given to their attorney for filing at the courthouse. However, they did not want the adoption to be printed in the Legal News at that time, so the document was kept in the attorney's office to be taken to the courthouse later. Years after when the attorney retired and cleaned out his files, my adoption record was found at the back of a file, still unrecorded at the Caddo Parish Office of Records. At that time, I was twenty-three years old, married, and the mother of three children.

I sat at the kitchen table that day and thought, "What if . . ."

A score of scenarios came up in my mind about all the things that could have happened to cause me to lose my connection to the only family I had ever known. Once again the attempt at secrecy did not keep me from receiving my rightful claims as a daughter. I never knew just why the adoption had to be kept from public knowledge at the time. I have since decided it must have been due to family in the area or perhaps to a person who might have found out he was a father and could have interfered with the process. In the end, nothing was lost. Once again the will of a Sovereign God was evident to me.

CHAPTER EIGHT

Seeing a Name

After talking with the cousins, I called all my children and told them I had some information that I wanted to pass on to them about my birth mother. When I visited Longview in August of 1992, I sat down with them to talk. They all agreed that it would not hurt anything to check out what I had heard. I talked with Ben Jr. by phone. He said, "Mom, I don't think it would be anything but positive for you to see what you can find out." With the approval of all of them and Ben's encouragement, I began again to pray about what to do.

During that visit, I decided to go to the Caddo Parish Court House and see what was on record there. Anna and Mark were free to make the trip with me, taking along Lindsey Camille, who was just about four months old. That day turned out to be one of the most emotional afternoons of my life.

We parked outside the court house and went to the second floor to the records room. I asked at the desk for help in locating an adoption record. When the clerk asked for a date and a name, I gave her April 7, 1959, which was the date when the papers were finally filed, and the name Tommie Brock. She went directly to a shelf, pulled down a large volume of Adoption Recordings, and looked in the index for Brock. She turned to a page and pushed the book toward me. To my amazement, Mona Lee Odom was the declared mother with the statement, "the father of said child is unknown to her." My knees turned to water. When I looked up, I saw the faces of Anna, Mark and Lindsey. I thanked God that I was not alone, and I realized once again how important my family is to me. None of us could believe that the information had been so attainable all these years. We asked for a copy of the document and within ten minutes had one in hand.

Sitting down with my three daughters at Anna's house, we read over the document and discussed the things we had come to know. It was an exciting time. We were all very speculative about the real facts. Ben and I had laughed and said if my mother's father was a judge or attorney in Baton Rouge in the late 30s, I might be kin to the Longs of Louisiana. After listening quietly and trying not to get into the conversation, my son-in-law Mark said, "Sounds like material for a TV movie to me!"

Two things stood out from this turn of events: (1) my birth mother only wanted to be sure that I was placed in a Christian home, and (2) at last I had a mother's name. If Mona Lee Odom was living in or near Shreveport when I was born, it is entirely possible that she remained in the area for some time, coming to see me and then passing by the house for several years after that. I wondered if she knew far more about me than I did about her since my wedding write-up was in the Shreveport paper with the names of my parents and family. My mother's obituary was also in the paper with my name and all the names of my children.

I began a search for the Odom family records. I followed the suggestion of adoption consultants and looked through census records at the Caddo Parish Library. There in the 1920 census was the Odom family, listing all the children of William Lee Odom. The last name was Mona Lee. Later Ben's mother saw in *The Shreveport Times* a small article inviting Odom relatives to attend a family reunion in New Orleans, Louisiana, that summer.

I contacted the Odom family reunion request, and one of the family members talked with me. At one point in our phone conversation, she turned to someone nearby and said, "Is Mona still alive?"

The answer was "Yes, she lives in Houston with her daughter."

That person mailed me a well-documented genealogy of the Odoms. The book contained the history of the four original Odom brothers who came west from South Carolina and settled in Union Parish, Louisiana, in the 1800s. There was a complete record of William Lee Odom with a short biography and a list of all his children with some addresses. I poured over the book one night so interested to read about all the ancestors of this Odom family. I felt I was beginning to know some of them.

Mother's words to Ben before our wedding were certainly true. William Lee Odom was an elected state representative in Louisiana. One child became a Louisiana Supreme Court Justice, adding a little truth to the story of a judge in my background. They were truly of a fine reputation. Grandfather Odom served as mayor of Bernice, Louisiana.

At the Thanksgiving season in 1992, Ben drove me to South Carolina, and we hunted for names and places of the Odoms who were forbears to those in Louisiana. We drove around in Barnwell, South Carolina, looking for a cemetery that might have the tombstones of those named in the Odom genealogy. We searched for a Rev. Darling Peeples because we were interested in his ministry. At the city cemetery, we found some caretakers and asked about a grave of the Rev. Darling Peeples. They knew of no one with that name, but said there was another cemetery outside of town. They gave us some brief directions, and we set out to find Rev. Peeples' resting place. We turned onto a dirt road and came to the end of it at a railroad track. There Ben drew a line – he was not taking his beloved used Cadillac across the tracks and on through a grassy trail to find another cemetery.

We did find out later that one of the Odoms had made the same trek before us. When they got home, they contacted the First Baptist Church of Barnwell where Rev. Peeples had been pastor for forty years, telling them of the condition of the grave and asking them to clean up the graves in respect for their former leader. Evidently, nothing was done since we could not find our way past the tracks.

Those third and fourth generation names just assured me that God's grace never fails. The threads of our lives are woven together in ways we never imagine. I had gained so much information about the Odoms. Yet once again, more questions were raised, and my search was not finished.

CHAPTER NINE

Breaking the Secret

In early 1994, Ben accepted the pastorate of First Baptist
Church in Hempstead, Texas, a small town north of
the Houston metro area. Again I was too busy to pursue the
trail I had started with the Odoms. But in early 1996, I asked
the church secretary if she had a Houston telephone directory.
She did and I looked for a name that I thought might be for
Mona Odom Foster. Finding nothing, I looked for the name of
her son-in-law, Mike Owen, who was listed in the genealogy.
Two Michaels and a Mike were listed. I gathered my courage,
breathed a prayer, and dialed the number for Mike Owen. I
got an answering machine, so I gave up and left no message.

The next Sunday evening, I tried again. This time the voice
of Mike Owen answered. I told him I was trying to reach Mona
Odom Foster. He said that was his mother-in-law who lived
right around the corner from him and his wife, Peg. Stunned
that I had made a connection, I asked about her health.

He said, "She's very healthy, but she smokes like a chim-
ney." He gave me her phone number. I mentioned that she was
acquainted with my mother in Shreveport, but said little else.

Finishing that call, I was trembling. I talked with Ben about what to do next. After discussing it for a good while, we decided it would be best to let someone else contact Mrs. Foster instead of me. We called our good friend, Dr. Sandee Williams, in Atlanta, Georgia, who was a Christian family counselor. I gave her the phone number for Mrs. Foster, and she said she would be happy to make a call on my behalf.

Minutes later our phone rang. It was Dr. Williams who had already spoken to Mrs. Foster. She told Mrs. Foster that she had a friend born on July 19, 1936, in Shreveport, who was trying to find her birth mother and perhaps Mrs. Foster was the right person.

Mrs. Foster's first question was, "What does she want?"

Sandee replied, "She is only trying to find out about her physical background for medical reasons."

"How do you know her," Mrs. Foster asked.

"My mother and Mrs. Rogers were best of friends, and she asked me to contact you on her behalf."

"I can't help you," was the reply. Sandee told her that my husband was a Baptist preacher near Houston, and she said, "Is that right?"

Dr. Williams ended the conversation, thanking her for her time. When Sandee called us back, she was convinced she had talked to my birth mother. The responses, suspicious attitude, and refusal to help all indicated we had found the right person.

Following up on the phone conversation, I decided to write a letter explaining the call and asking once again if she might be my birth mother who willingly gave me up for adoption sixty years before. Mrs. Foster was almost eighty-two years old at this point, and I was about to have my sixtieth birthday. I tried as respectfully as I could to tell her about my questions, a little about who I was, what my life had been like, and about my wonderful family. The letter went off, and I began to wait for the reply I hoped for.

A month passed. Then one day, I walked to the mailbox to find a beautifully, handwritten letter with the forwarding address from Mrs. Foster's address on Wunderlich in Houston. These are the words I read:

Dear Nita,

Thank you for your letter of some weeks ago. I'm sorry to be so late in replying, but at my age (coming up on my eighty-second birthday) I am inclined to procrastinate.

When I received the phone call from Ms. Williams, I was in a thorough state of shock. All I could think of was that this was an unscrupulous person pulling a scam on me. After receiving your letter, I knew better. Please apologize to her for me if I seemed rude. It is not my nature to be rude.

I will fill you in to some extent as to how I handled this sad and almost unbelievable episode in my young life. It might be hard for you to believe, but never in the past sixty years have I ever told anyone about this chapter in my life, including my beloved daughter and other members of my family. After seeking God's help and consulting with a couple of professionals in this line, I was convinced that I was doing the right thing. After meeting with your parents for the one time, I was even more convinced.

If any of my family has ever been told of my indiscreet and immature actions of so long ago, they love me enough to respect my decision for silence, and I would like to keep it that way.

To get on with a brief synopsis of my life afterward, shortly before the United States got into the Second World War, I met and later married my beloved husband. After the war, we started our odyssey of about twenty years of living in different sections of the United States and Canada. During this time, our daughter Peg was born. I continued traveling with my husband until she was ready to enter school, and needless to say, I had to stay put. We chose Salt Lake City where we had lived for a year or so and where we had discussed retiring to when the time came as we all loved that part of our country. But, what is the saying, "man proposes but God disposes." So true – my husband died prematurely and rather suddenly when he was on a business trip on the East Coast. I was with him and brought his body back to Texas, the land of his birth. I have been a widow for over thirty two years.

When I made the decision to return to the Southland, I also thought it would be wise to get back in the work force as I still had seven or eight years of my daughter's education to see to. We made it, and she graduated

*with honors from the University of Houston in Fashion
Merchandising. For eighteen or twenty years, she made
many trips to different places in the world on buying
trips for large department stores. This much travel was
about to get the best of her, so she decided to go into the
selling end. She is now a factory representative which
requires no foreign travel and likes it real well. Her husband is also in this business with a different company.
They are away from home quite a lot, and I look after
their home for them.*

*It sounds as though you and your family have had a
wonderful life together, beginning with your childhood.
It sounds like God has richly blessed you for your dili-
gence in His work. I, too, was raised in a strictly religious
home. My father was for over forty years a deacon in the
Baptist church. Also, three of my brothers served in this
capacity in their respective churches. When we married,
my husband was a Methodist and I a Baptist. In order
to compromise, we decided when my daughter was of the
age to have her instruction in the faith and doctrines of
the Presbyterian Church (age twelve), and we would all
go into the Presbyterian at once since we had attended
the church and liked it. So she was baptized, and we all
joined. We are pleased with it.*

*God has blessed me with good health, considering my
age, and I am thankful. I am a very independent soul
and have been always. I pray I can stay that way. I am at
peace within myself and hope to stay that way.*

I wish for you and your family many more years of happiness and family love and His love.

Most sincerely,

Mona O. Foster

P.S. From the picture of you and your Ben, I would say that you are a handsome couple. Thanks.

What a beautiful expression of her handling of the "sad and almost unbelievable episode" in her life. That episode was me! Her writing displayed her intelligence, kind spirit, tough and independent personality, and loyalty to her own family. Her vocabulary and English construction were wonderful. I was impressed with this senior adult and the trials she had faced at many stages in her life. So many questions were still unanswered, but she had shared some deep thoughts with me.

CHAPTER TEN

Making a Connection

The beautifully crafted letter caused my heart to race. I began to ask God to tell me what to do next. Some days later, I made my own phone call to Mrs. Foster. She spoke in a quiet voice. I detected no surprise or anxiety in her tone. I expressed my appreciation for her nice letter and said how hard it must have been to write.

She replied, "Yes, it was hard, Nita, very hard. Sixty years is a long time."

We talked about her independence and that she hoped she could stay that way. I shared with her that I too am very independent, and I have three daughters who are also very independent. I asked if I could come to meet her and have lunch sometime. She said it would have to be when her children (Peg and Mike) were out of town, but she would think about it.

I was very emotionally shaken by her voice and her gentleness to me. When I ended our conversation, I said, "I'm not sure how you will take this, but I want to wish you a Happy Mother's Day."

Her answer was, "Well, darling, I hope you have a good vacation." I promised to call again.

On Ben's day off, we drove to Houston and found her apartment. Ben wanted to stop and meet her, but I was too unsure about all the events, so we just passed by. She was no more than forty-five minutes away from me. My hope began to grow that she would meet me and get acquainted.

When we got back from vacation, I called her once again to ask about a meeting. Her attitude was wonderful, but she again declined to meet, saying it would be too upsetting at this time in her life. I respected her answer even though I was greatly disappointed.

In that final conversation, I told her that Mother had never talked to me about my adoption and lived in almost total denial that I was adopted. I told her how long it was before the signed adoption decree was filed at the Caddo Parish Courthouse. She seemed surprised and then went on to say that she and mother had an oral pact never to tell anyone. At the time, she said she had no job, no money, and such a situation was very unacceptable then. She could not share such news with her wonderful family, who, she said, never knew. She said that if they did, they never talked to her about it, so she agreed to the adoption.

She told me the father never knew, and she was sure he was deceased by now. As I had suspected, my biological father was not unknown. She refused to answer my question to name my biological father. I asked her if he was in any way connected with my adoptive family as my cousin had speculated.

"Absolutely not," was Mona's reply. "It sounds like they are trying to pry into your business." I thanked her for setting that to rest for me.

She said she was sorry Mother didn't talk to me more about this. I expressed my respect and great admiration for her decision. I also told her I felt adoption was so much better than single parenting. She agreed heartily. I said I believed that *God works all things...* and she took up the verse and finished it, *for good to those who love Him* (Romans 8:28). I was completely overwhelmed that I could share God's Word with this woman who was such a great unknown element in my life. She made the statement that she got the feeling that Mother would not have wanted me to do this. I answered that my mother was my greatest supporter, and she would have understood.

We talked fifteen or twenty minutes. I asked about grandchildren. She said she had none. I asked if I could send some questions for her to answer for me, and she said that might be all right. I did draft the questions, but decided against sending them. That was our last personal contact. It was early May of 1996. At this point, two mothers had opened up to me about their secret.

My first reaction at the close of that phone call was utter dismay. I said, "She intends to die with this information that is so important to me still a secret." I felt I was standing before a door that had just been slammed in my face. Of all the facts a child should have, it seems to me that the names of her parents should be at the top of the list. Their genetic makeup determined what and who I would be. Their blood flows in my veins, and their physical characteristics are reproduced in me and in my children. What is a bloodline for if it is not to give identity to a person?

After years of not even knowing I was adopted, having others talk about my adoption behind my back, and feeling as if others knew something about me that I did not, I was still in the dark about the most intimate facts of my life. As Mona said, "Sixty years is a long time."

I am so grateful that I know Who my Heavenly Father is. He has never lied to me, turned away my questions and longings, and loves me unconditionally. I was truly disappointed and frustrated. I tried to fill in the blanks for me and for my children, but in 1996 I was stymied by the well-kept secret of these two mothers. However, it is true *by the grace of God I am what I am* (1 Corinthians 15:10).

Thinking about the circumstances of Mona's life at that time, I considered the fact that my mother would probably have responded the same way. She was in her eighties, and I recalled how Mother reacted to events and changes in her life when she was in her eighties. I would not have wanted some stranger to walk into her life and cause an emotional upheaval. I do not blame Mrs. Foster for backing away and refusing to go through such a trauma. However, I had made contact with her and began to pray about future contacts.

CHAPTER ELEVEN

Closing the Door

*W*e moved back to our home in Jacksonville, Florida, after that. Ben returned to teaching at Luther Rice Seminary and to his travel and evangelistic work. I went back to work for the Florida Baptist State Convention offices. I continued to send cards, letters, and pictures to Mrs. Foster. Since my children were her only grandchildren, I hoped she would enjoy seeing their pictures and knowing something about them. I never received any response nor had any mail returned. I assumed she was still living at the Houston address on Wunderlich, but was never sure just what happened to the cards and letters I sent her on Mother's Day, her birthday in June, and Christmas.

My last letter was after we retired and moved back to Longview in April 2002. I told her we were back in Texas, had retired, and were enjoying the grandchildren and visits from the children. Still there was no response. My last effort was a card at Christmas 2002, wishing her good health and once again saying how grateful I was to her. What did she do with my mail? Was it stored away out of the view of her children, or did she crumple it up and toss it into a wastebasket? I would never know.

Each spring I remembered that the years had passed, now almost seven, since I first made contact with Mrs. Foster. In February 2003, I said to myself, "I will never know whether she is dead or alive. She's going to her grave with the information I want." A month later, we started taking the Longview News-Journal again, just to keep up with the local news and sales, work the crosswords, and use in the fireplace, I guess.

On Sunday March 9, while reading the obituaries, I was stunned to see the obituary for Mona Lee Odom Foster, whose funeral was scheduled for the next afternoon at 2:00 p.m. Of course, I knew all about the Odom family, but could hardly believe that she was to be buried beside her husband in a cemetery in Gladewater – thirty minutes from me. My emotions really went berserk. She was dead, and like I had known all along, she carried every answer I wanted with her into eternity. She never talked with me about her pregnancy, nor answered the one question I had about my father.

There was no question but that Ben and I would attend the funeral, although it was a little unnerving to think about walking in on that family not knowing who would be there. We scrubbed up, dressed up, and drove to Croley Funeral Home in Gladewater. After signing the guest registry, we went down the aisle of the chapel to look into the face of the woman who sixty-six years before gave me life and gave me up to a family. She was petite and had long fingers that were noticeably bent from arthritis. She was dressed in a two-piece, teal-colored dress, my favorite color.

Ben looked at her and said, "Nita, there's your nose."

It was all I could do to whisper under my breath, "Thank you."

There were pictures of Mrs. Foster with her husband and daughter, Peg. A large, antique-framed picture of the nine Odom children hung above the casket.

We went back near the rear of the chapel and sat down. I looked around and listened to pick up names of the people there. Some obviously looked like her – short and dark-haired. Once two of the pallbearers stood near Ben in the aisle and almost spoke to him, but they were distracted and walked away.

I had my answer ready – Mrs. Foster and my mother were friends when I was born. Following that, I didn't know what to expect, but we never had to talk to anyone.

Down the aisle came a young woman in her mid-fifties, carrying a tote bag with burgundy-colored feathers around the top edge. I nudged Ben and said, "That's Peg." As it turned out, that was Peg. According to Mrs. Foster's letter in previous pages, Peg had a degree in Fashion Merchandising from the University of Houston so I had expected her to be a little trendy. She was.

The funeral began with a blonde lady in her fifties and possibly her son who sang "How Great Thou Art." I watched Peg sitting on the front row with her husband, Mike Owen, mouthing the words and singing along with them. Then the chaplain from the funeral home read from John 11, the same verses that so comforted me when Mollie died, and also John 14. Then the young man came back and sang "The Wind Beneath My Wings." At that point, the chaplain turned the service over to Peg for remarks. What followed was incredible to me.

Reading from prepared notes in a red file folder, she began by saying Mona was the last child born, the last child married, and the last child to have a child, and now she was the last of the nine Odom children to die. She painted a portrait of her mother's personality, interests, and family. Her mother had taught her so much about life, she said. One of her mother's quotes was, "Sometimes you have to laugh to keep from crying."

Peg said Mona was a good "glarer." In the hospital the last week of her life, Mona raised the blanket between her and Peg to hide and pulled the oxygen tube out, proving again how independent and stubborn she was. Grandmother Odom said that Mona was the only one of her children that she never understood. When Peg took her to the doctor last summer, it was the first time in thirty years that she had been to a doctor, even though she was a chain smoker all her life. The doctor told Peg she had a good set of genes. As I learned later, she had been living in an assisted living place and was two years into Alzheimer's. Still I didn't learn where all the mail was going that I had sent.

Peg also read letters written by her father to her mother around 1937-1939. He had a drinking problem. Peg and her mother lived in Salt Lake City, and her father, Morriss Foster, worked on the East Coast in New York. Suddenly in 1962, he became very ill, and they were called to New York. He died three weeks later. Following that, Mona and Peg moved to Gladewater. Peg graduated from high school in Gladewater. She and Mona moved to Nacogdoches, Texas, where Peg attended Stephen F. Austin State University and then on to Houston where she earned her degree. She said Mona was very close to three of her sisters who lived in Gladewater and in Shreveport.

Peg said her mother was her yard boy, bringing flats of flowers and fertilizer to plant her beds for her. She also said Mona loved people, even remaining friends with Peg's exes.

Mike said she was a great lady, "She never once pissed me off."

Peg's last remark was, "My mother taught me everything I needed to know, except how to live without her."

When she finished, she asked for several of her cousins to come and talk about the family. For another hour, we listened to five of them tell everything imaginable about the Odom family from Union Parish, Louisiana. First we heard of the grandparents who married in 1895 and raised a family of five boys and four girls. Mona, born in 1914, was a vital member of a lovely family. Grandpa William Lee Odom led by example. Following his time in the state legislature, he came back to Bernice and became mayor. The heritage was not of worldly goods, but of Christian values, education, and public service.

The next family member to speak was a niece, daughter of the Mona's oldest brother, Marion. She was only a few years younger than Mona. She reminded the crowd that their uncle Fred Odom was a Supreme Court Justice in Louisiana. I learned that Mona's nickname was "Cush," but no one knew why. She said they knew that Uncle Henry, Aunt Dana, and Grandma Odom would be the first at the church when the doors were opened at First Baptist, Bernice. She spoke of the large home of the grandparents in Bernice where there was a piano in the parlor that anyone could play anytime. She said the family was known by a great sense of humor and their generous, giving spirit. She told that Mona graduated from high school in Bernice at fifteen. She also remembered that once when she came to visit, she brought two beautiful new dresses for her.

Following the niece, Mona's oldest nephew spoke. He said it was a joy to be with Mona (no one called her Aunt Mona). There was a special bond between the sisters. This was interesting because if Mona was so close to her three sisters, it is hard to imagine that none of them knew of Mona's pregnancy or the adoption like she had told me. He explained that his pastor now lives in the house that Mona built when she moved back to Gladewater. He gave a clear presentation of the gospel, saying that Mona had asked Jesus Christ into her heart, and if we did, then we could know that we would be together again. This was one of the questions I had hoped to answer – that my birth mother was a Christian. That means I will see her in heaven one day.

Continuing the family history, another nephew spoke of his mother, Polly, and Uncle Van Odom. Uncle Van was a fastidious dresser and a top-notch educator. I knew that he was a principal in Haynesville, but then he became Superintendent of Schools in Monroe. He made the point that they were a diverse selection of characters, and it seemed that when each child married, he/she brought another character to fill in the gaps in the family. They sounded so much like my own precious clan. He told of how Uncle Billy would come to family gatherings, and the kids would hear glasses clinking in the kitchen. Someone always asked him if he had brought the "household goods" which was code for the "hard stuff."

The last to speak was another niece from south Louisiana.

Peg had asked her to tell something about her mother, Tressie, and her uncle, J. Y. Odom. She said Tressie loved music and sang in the choir of First Baptist, Tallulah, Louisiana. That's where Daddy was working when Ben and I went to ask if we could get married. The youngest son, JY (Jared Young, named for a Louisiana Republican governor) and his wife, Betty, whose real name was Margaret, lived in a big house on Dudley Drive in Shreveport. This niece and her twin sister would go stay with them often. Tressie was known in the family as a fun-loving gal. Once at Mother's, I found a letter from someone named Margaret, asking Mother to contact her. When I asked Mother about it, she wouldn't say anything, but pretended not to remember. Later, I went back for the letter, and it was gone. I believe it must have been a letter from JY's wife there in Shreveport, attempting to contact me or my family.

Ben said he never saw anyone take notes at a funeral, but I did. At the end of the family history, the blonde lady sang "The Old Rugged Cross," and the chaplain led in prayer. Once again we filed by the casket to take a last look at Mona Odom Foster. I was almost too stunned to react emotionally. All I could say was that God had planned this entire service for my benefit. What an awesome God we serve. He has directed every step of my life. When I praise Him, I have to begin nine months before I was born. Now here I was at the funeral of someone I actually never knew, but there was clearly connection. I can hardly believe how this came to be – only by the grace of God. The secret that these two mothers had so faithfully kept all these years was finally open for my heart to ponder.

At last it seemed my journey through all these doors had

come to a conclusion. God let me look at the face of my birth mother and learn she was a Christian. I don't know if she had looked at me or held me in her arms in those brief days before she gave me up. I did understand what it might have been like since I, too, had given up a precious infant daughter years before. A mother's heart carries so many emotions. Loss of a child is, perhaps, the hardest to bear.

Chapter Twelve

Making Sense
of a Funeral

*S*itting down days later to reflect on the funeral led me
to some personal observations. I realized that my life
had been touched by two mothers. I had come to know them
both, to appreciate each one's place in my life, and to accept
their individuality. Now I had experienced the funerals of both
of these mothers. How awesome to know the hand of God had
kept us apart, yet brought us together in due time even if it had
been sixty years. Mona had quoted for me Romans 8:28 when we
spoke on our first phone conversation: *All things work together*
for good to those who love God. She had quoted another saying:
"Man proposes, but God disposes." I think this was her way
of saying how she had dealt with this issue in her life. She had
come to believe it was all what God "disposed."

It was obvious that in the biological family, I had a godly,
loving, generous, and talented heritage. The Odoms were a well-
known and fine family, the best of citizens as well as church-goers.
In her letter, she informed me that her brothers were Baptist

deacons and hers was a family that knew God's Word and loved His church. Though Mona left her Baptist church when she left home, she re-established the connection as a Presbyterian after Peg was born. The cousins who now carry on the heritage seem to be the "keepers of the castle." They are proud of their ancestors and believe them to be unique and special.

Watching Peg that day, I felt that she was surrounded by a host of kin who are her support system. She impressed me as a very confident, successful, and capable woman. She also seems to be open and happy. Our lives had moved through different experiences, and I was content for both of us to stay on our own courses.

Ben graciously sat with me throughout the service, listening to them talk of all the love in the Odom family. Later he said he wanted to stand up and say, "If you're such a loving family, I'd like to introduce you to a family member you have never known." Thank God, he did not do that. But we talked for a long time about what God had done that day.

Since God put such an awesome closure on Mona Odom Foster for me, I believed at that time He wanted me to shut the door on my search. As I concluded these notes from Mona's funeral, that is what I wanted to do.

I have a family – no less loving, talented, generous, and godly than the Odoms that I heard about at that funeral. I have never needed for one thing in my life – physically, emotionally, or spiritually. I am sorry that these people have never known my family, but I am determined not to bring any reproach or disappointment into that family about their beloved aunt

Mona, or into Peg's life regarding the mother that she so loved and cherished.

The biological tendencies of the Odoms surely show in my genes – in my love for music, writing, love of people, humor, wit, their close-knit family ties, and even their love for the church. The tension between heritage and environment was and still is evident in my life and my extended family. At last I had some evidence from my ancestors that I really could see in my own children and grandchildren.

Finally, I want to say to those who read this, God rules and He overrules. Never let your past victories or failures keep you from pressing on in your life to love, encourage, pray for, and support your parents, your children, grandchildren, friends, and co-workers. Serve God wherever He puts you to your very best ability with His help. What you are is far more important than what you do or where you came from. God's will is *good, and acceptable, and perfect* (Romans 12:2). He works all things together for good (Rom. 8:28). His amazing grace planned your life beginning nine months before you took your first breath in this world. You are truly a gift of His grace.

Human pride is a strange thing. Even though my adoption was a very unselfish act by Mrs. Foster, she still had hung on to her desire for secrecy. My mother too failed to share the details and emotions she had dealt with before, during, and after my arrival. Neither of them was totally honest in all the details of their decisions. It is true that in spite of all the answers I found, more questions came to mind.

I am not a crusader for open record adoptions. Today most adoptions are matters of record between an agency and the mother and adoptive parents. Some birth mothers even survey prospective parents for their babies, meet them, share the baby's birth, and keep in touch with mutual consent. I believe a child should have every chance for stability, security, and acceptance. However, there comes a time when the facts should be made available, especially to an adult adoptee. An agency should be required to open the records to the one whose life has been redirected by adoption. In my case, private adoption procedures between the parties and an attorney took place. If I had not looked up the records, I would never have even had a mother's name. The individuals who had the facts were not willing to share them, even with me.

When the facts are known, they may be unpleasant; however, each of us has a right to know about our birth parents, good or bad. It may be that, in fact, the father is unknown because of the mother's lifestyle or because of his denial or total indifference. Some go so far as to look for DNA evidence of birth connections. Nevertheless, when names are known and requested, I believe an adoptee should be told and allowed to deal with the truth openly.

Whatever the circumstances surrounding an adoption, the most important fact is that at some point a pregnant woman made one incredible decision: she chose life. To look beyond the problems and questions about continuing a pregnancy and to decide to give yourself to nurturing and delivering that child, even if it means hardship and personal sacrifice, is one of life's greatest choices. Moses left the children of Israel with these words: *I have set before you life and death . . . therefore choose life, that both you and your descendants may live . . . and that you may cling to Him, for He is your life* (Deuteronomy 30:19-20).

CHAPTER THIRTEEN

That Wasn't the End

At the death of Mona Odom Foster I considered the story closed. It was a while before I put all I had felt into perspective. It was an amazing conclusion, I thought. Periodically, Ben would say, "Don't you think you need to contact your sister?"

"Why," I would answer. "She has a busy and successful life and has no idea I even exist. Why rock her boat?" I felt that since Peg was twelve years younger than me, still working, married to Mike, her third husband, with no children, we had little in common.

That attitude ended about 4:30 a.m. Saturday morning on Memorial Day weekend of 2008. I woke up with one thought on my mind – "Write Peg." I went right then to the computer and wrote a lengthy letter, trying to be as tactful and sensitive as I could be. I read and reread it and then put it in the mail. The letter read:

Dear Margaret,

This letter is in regard to your mother, Mona Lee Odom Foster, who passed away more than five years ago. Please

*know that I am very hesitant to share the information in
this letter. It is not my intent to upset or cause you confusion or hurt.*

*Enclosed is a copy of the Caddo Parish Court Record
of an adoption that took place in July of 1936 between
Mona Lee Odom and my adoptive parents, Minnie and
Tommie Brock of Shreveport. It has taken me this long
to share this event with you, and I would not do it now
except I really feel God is leading me to closure in this
matter.*

*My adoptive mother died in 1989, and I began to search
for my biological roots. This is a long story, but led me to
your mother in 1996. My husband, Dr. Ben Rogers, was
pastor of First Baptist Church, Hempstead, Texas, when
I located Mrs. Foster and discovered she had a daughter.
My initial phone call was to Mike Owen to enquire about
Mrs. Foster. He shared that she was in good health and
lived near you. I then asked a Christian counselor friend
to call her and try to gently ask about July 1936. Your
mother was very suspicious, as she should have been,
and closed the conversation by saying she could not be of
any help in my search. Following the phone call, convinced that she was the person I was looking for, I wrote
a letter telling her about my life, family, and desire just
to get more information about my physical background.
Almost a month later, I received a beautiful handwritten letter from her, telling me very little about my birth,
but telling me all about her life, marriage, and so much*

about you. A typical devoted mother! She told me in the letter that no one in her family knew of this, and she and my mother had agreed never to speak about it. My mother kept her bargain. I never knew I was adopted until some kids at school told me. It's hard to believe no one in the Odom family was aware of this. I will be happy to share a copy of the letter with you if you would like to see it.

I made a couple of phone calls and spoke with her and had asked her to let me take her to lunch or coffee to get acquainted. She said she would think about it, but when I called back, she declined, saying she was not willing to get emotionally involved in a new relationship. I respected her decision.

We moved from Texas to Florida that summer of 1996, and I began to contact her by mail on special occasions, sending pictures of Ben and me, our children, and grandchildren. I never got any response back from her and have wondered how she handled my correspondence.

In March of 2003, we had retired and moved back to Longview, and to my amazement, I read one Sunday of her death and the funeral that would be in Gladewater. My husband and I attended the funeral. It was the first time I had ever seen her in person, and it was a very surreal experience for me. The service itself was most revealing about all your family, and I recognized you immediately from the little your mother had shared. I said nothing to anyone and came home feeling I had closed that book.

My husband has encouraged me to get in touch with you. I have felt until now that I didn't need to bother your life, and my life has been so blessed and full that I have not needed another relationship either. However, this morning about 4 o'clock, I believe the Lord woke me to lead me to write to you. I know your mother's birthday is near, and I thought maybe you would be coming to east Texas to visit family this summer. If you feel that you can respond to this news, I would be happy to meet you. If you do not want to deal with this, I totally understand and pray nothing but God's best for you.

Please know that I have shared this connection with no one personally. I have told the amazing story of my "Two Mothers," but never mentioned names of your family who live in this area. Since I grew up in Shreveport, I know I must have brushed the lives of several through the years.

Peg, please give this information your thoughtful consideration. Let me know how you feel, and I promise that whatever you think should be done will be perfectly acceptable to me.

Deepest regards, Nita

What kind of an answer, if any, would I get? Would Peg be suspicious, angry, embarrassed, or what? A day or so later, the phone rang, and the voice on the other end was Peg's. When she had come in from work, her husband, Mike, told her that she'd better sit down and read a letter she had received. In tears, she began to tell me what a thrill it had been to find out she had a sister. At that point, she assured me that she had nothing but the greatest reaction to the information I had told her in the letter. We talked for more than an hour. She shared that every day for five years she had cried, thinking she was all alone. She and her mother were very close, and Peg had no children. Actually, when I thought about it, she got a lot more than she bargained for when she came into the Rogers' clan. To say nothing of falling into a nest of Baptists – and preachers, at that!

Chapter Fourteen

Adding a Little Sister

Following Peg's absolute delight in finding out about me, we had several conversations. The next step, of course, was actually meeting each other. We arranged that she and Mike would come to Longview for a visit the weekend of my seventy-second birthday in July. It was an emotional time as we prepared to meet them. Since Peg had passed her news on to the Odom cousins with positive responses, we decided to invite the cousins who lived in the area to join us. Peg and Mike came for lunch with only Ben and me. Later that afternoon the others joined us.

The only one of our children who came was Anna with her husband Mark. I had a special birthday cake made to celebrate "A special day," not just a birthday. The cousins who lived in the Longview area came and were very kind. Of course, there was lots of curiosity from all of us about my addition to the "Odoms." For the five years now following that day, we have called July 19 "Sister Day." Mike summed up the effect of all of this on Peg when he said, "It's good to see you smile again."

Peg and Mike jumped into our family wholeheartedly, and

our children were happy to get to know her. She loved each of them, all the grandchildren, and great-grandchildren added to the circle of family. During the Labor Day weekend, we had another get-together when all our children came for barbecue at our son's lake house on Lake O' the Pines. What a great event – not a reunion, but a union of the two of us. Now I am "Big Sis" and Peg is "Little Sis." I love to introduce her as my five-year-old sister.

To my amazement Peg began to send photographs and stories about Mona. The physical likeness between us was undeniable! She and Mike noticed similarities in our facial expressions, humor, and size. I learned that Peg had pleaded for years for a brother. So had I for many years. Peg and I had both grown up as only children, although from the same mother. Both of us enjoyed the attention, encouragement, and faithful love as only a single child would.

I learned that Mona would play every piano she saw. Peg gave me a picture of the choir at First Baptist, Bernice, with Grandmother Odom among the singers. Music was big with the Odoms as it has been with the Rogers. Mona loved children, animals, and get-togethers.

The similarities between Mona and my mother were uncanny. Both had followed their husbands as work moved them from place to place. Both poured themselves into the one daughter each had. Both were widowed for many years and proudly lived independently. Both were loyal to their families, siblings, nieces and nephews. Both had died just a few months before their ninetieth birthdays.

Mona had lived in Shreveport with one of her sisters. When

we visited Ben's family, we drove right by the gingerbread-trimmed house where she lived. She also lived in Gladewater with another sister. Our son-in-law served on the church staff at First Baptist Church of Gladewater where Mona's sister and family attended. They were well known at the church when he was youth minister there. At one time, Mona lived in Longview at the same time mother was living with us. I am sure that throughout my life, our paths almost crossed.

I have found my sister to be another loving and generous person. She has shared some of Mona's furniture with me and an emerald ring that she gave to Mona that Mona wore every day. We have developed a real Sister Day, exchanging cards and calls. Peg makes an effort to be involved in the activities of the expanding Rogers tribe. She comes on holidays, comes to baby showers, birthday parties, and has become Aunt Peg to all the family. Mike and Ben Jr. are enjoying hunting together. Now Peg has a brother-in-law she refers to as Ben-in-law. Ben's mother has loved getting to know her. She had a part in helping me make Odom contacts in Shreveport, so she feels a part of this story – and she is. Brother-in-law Mike expressed it well when he said, "It's a shame Mona didn't live to see how much joy Nita has brought to Peg."

Peg attends church with us and even sits in my Bible study class and listens to me teach. Her Presbyterian background was different from all the Baptists in my family. She keeps searching the hymnal for songs she remembers. Today's Bible translations are new to her because she knows only King James verses. Peg's school years were spent in Salt Lake City where she and Mona were active in a Presbyterian church. Their pastor made a great impression for God on Peg. He was the one who came to school to tell Peg that her father had died. The caption on a coffee mug that Peg gave me tells the truth about the two of us: "We are sisters: same blood, totally different planets."

As Peg and I continue to visit and share our experiences, I am more and more amazed at this story. I have been surprised at the reaction of so many people touched by this story – relatives, friends who had no clue that I was adopted, and people who themselves have searched out their own adoption stories. I once was asked by a friend who had an adopted son, "How did your folks handle your adoption so you became such a happy person?"

My reply was, "They did everything wrong related to my adoption, but God kept me on the right track." Mine is the story of two Christian mothers who were committed to their agreement, promising to keep their mutual love for a small baby in their hearts and refusing to break their pact with each other for more than sixty years. It is a very intriguing tale, one I could not make up in a thousand years.

CHAPTER FIFTEEN

Knowing a Father

*T*his story would not be complete if I did not address the issue of my unknown father. Every child needs a father who will provide security and love for her. Some adopted children have a hard time getting past not knowing who that biological father is. This is so understandable and natural. I would like to have had just a name to fill that blank, but I never will. The only person that I believe had that knowledge is now gone. I did my best to get some information, but my biological mother never provided it. I do not believe that the answer she put on my adoption record, "Father unknown," was the actual truth. She did not live such a promiscuous life that her "sad and unbelievable episode" was just another event. I truly believe she knew the father, saying in her letter that "he never knew," but she chose to withhold that name either in her own interest or in his. That being said, how have I come to handle the unknown in my life?

Two major truths give me perfect peace about this. One is the wonderful, loving, hard-working father that I knew for the first eighteen years of my life. Tommie Brock dearly loved me. He and I spent time together in the yard, at the gas station, and on the roads as we traveled. During the summer months, mother and I spent days on his jobs, watching him drill wells in north Louisiana and east Texas. It was a thrill to me to go up on the floor of the rig and hold the wheel that guided all that pipe into the ground. His crew was friendly and loved watching Daddy and me on the job. I loved even the smell of that rig and still get teary-eyed when I drive past an oil or gas well at night and see the derrick lit up.

Daddy was a man's man. He was the middle son who had been sickly as a child. His mother was very protective and did not insist that he go to school since he was "poorly" in health. As a result, he never learned to read or write. I never knew this until I was in high school. I watched him many times add a double column of numbers for his reports on the job. And when the Sunday papers came, I would see him "read" the comics. Actually, he was looking at the drawings. His sparse education kept him from accepting promotions that required more reading and writing skills than he had.

He had worked as a "mule-skinner" in the woods of north Louisiana early in life. He worked on pipelines, drilled oil wells, worked through the depression, and many times was paid in mineral rights on property rather than in cash. His jobs afforded him no Social Security, health insurance, or retirement benefits, but he always had money in his wallet. He paid cash for the house he had built and cash for a 1953 Buick Super that he gave Mother and me. Once when his knee was crushed by the pressure of a water pump blow-out on the job, he lost six months of work. How we met our expenses, I never knew. I remember his boss, J. I. Roberts, coming to the house and giving Mother some money to help with the hospital expense.

Daddy had some special habits: he always drove a Ford for

his work car, never cursed in front of me, opened our home for Mother's relatives during World War II, never came home drunk, though he did have a drink occasionally on the way home from a job. He was a chain smoker, going through two or three packs a day. He bought cigarettes by the carton and would light a new cigarette from the stub of the last one. This was his downfall. Working hard in all kinds of weather in his starched khakis, he pushed his heart and lungs too hard, and it shortened his life.

He could smoke a cigarette down to his very lip before dropping it and stepping on it. He had smoking down to a fine art. Of course, he had some burnt places in his khakis and on the back seat of his car where the ashes blew back into the back window. I recall his chronic cough. Those were days before a warning was printed on cigarette packages, and doctors warned us that smoking could cause lung cancer.

Shortly after Ben and I married, my Daddy died of a sudden and massive heart attack. I had seen him endure his first attack about seven years before, but this was a total surprise to Mother and to me. He and Mother had been out to dinner with friends to celebrate Mother's birthday in 1955. He turned the key in the ignition of the car; the car lurched, and he fell back dead as the victim of a second heart attack.

It was months before I got over losing my daddy. Mother also took it very hard. It was so sudden for both of us. I had Ben, and we were expecting our first child, but Mother felt all alone. Daddy never knew any of his grandchildren. I have often said they would have been spoiled rotten if he had been around. For months, I would pray and ask the Lord to tell Daddy that I missed him and that I was all right. My only earthly father was gone, but I knew where he was.

Once after Ben came into the family, Daddy said he wanted to show Ben something. He pulled out his wallet and took out a small folded piece of paper. As he carefully unfolded it, it made the shape of a cross. It was Daddy's way of telling Ben, the preacher, that he had placed his faith in what Jesus did on that cross, and it was important. Daddy heard Ben preach several times before his death. He said one day to Mother, "Does that boy have more than one sermon?" Seems that each time Daddy went to hear Ben preach, he preached about Zacchaeus up in the sycamore tree. I think Daddy could have preached that sermon himself.

The second major truth is that I still have a Father, the sovereign God of the universe. He has been in my life personally since I was eight years old. When I received Jesus, God's Son, into my heart, God the Father as well as God the Holy Spirit came to live in me – not just with me, but in me. He is a Father to all who call upon Him in truth, the Bible says. He provides me with perfect love and total security. He will be a Father to anyone who feels that they have no father or that their earthly father really doesn't care about them or love them.

God, my Father, loves me with an everlasting love. He has the answer to all my questions and the problems I face. He will never leave me, nor forsake me. He has solved the problem of sin and has forgiven me for every sin, past, present and future. He sent His one and only Son to pay the price for my sin and make me righteous in God's eyes for now and all eternity.

I believe knowing God as my Father was the bedrock of security I needed to face the facts – known and unknown – of my adoption. Trusting Jesus Christ as my personal Savior gave me forgiveness, acceptance, and purpose for my life.

CHAPTER SIXTEEN

Twice Born,
Twice Adopted

*W*hen Ben reminds me that he is his mother's only son, I love to remind him that his folks had to take what they got, but I was a chosen child. He also tells people that "Nita is the best argument against abortion that I know." To give life to an innocent unborn is to realize that all life is a gift from God, Who is Life. As Job said, *The Lord gave, and the Lord has taken away; Blessed be the name of the Lord* (Job 1:21). An unselfish decision to bring a new life with all its potential for good into the world is a choice that can bring unknown blessings to the lives of all involved.

Everyone has the experience of birth – it's the only way to become a part of the human family. Great attention is being given in today's world to all the possible ways couples can become parents: invitro fertilization, surrogate mothers, as well as adoption. Looming on the horizon is the possibility of cloning human beings. Still, it is true that a person must be born physically in some fashion to take his place in society. I want to add also that there still are just two kinds of babies born into this world – boys and girls. Some scientists have pushed the idea of a biological reason for homosexual individuals. The truth remains that opposite sexes produce new life. Though a homosexual couple desires to be a family, they still must depend on someone outside their relationship to provide them with children. God is the great Designer of families. His plan is perfect.

Everyone also has the potential of a second birth. The Bible makes this truth so clear in the story of Nicodemus and his night visit to Jesus. In John 3, their visit is recorded. Nicodemus was stunned by Jesus' statement "You must be born again (or from above)."

The intelligent, respected, Jewish scholar replied like any human would: "How can this be? Can a man go back into his mother's womb and be born?" Jesus made it clear that a second birth was provided only by the Holy Spirit through faith in the Son of God.

And then Jesus spoke what I believe is the greatest verse in Scripture: *For God so loved the world that He gave His only begotten Son, that whosoever believeth in Him should not perish, but have everlasting life* (John 3:16 KJV). It was hard for Nicodemus to grasp the truth of a second birth, but he evidenced his belief in Jesus when he openly claimed Jesus' dead body and helped with his burial.

I was born the first time on a July day in 1936, but I was born a second time in the summer of 1944 when by faith I asked Jesus Christ to forgive my sin and receive me as His child. What a wonderful privilege to be one of God's children and a part of His universal body of believers.

In my case, too, I have been adopted twice. That first adoption was also in July 1936, but as you have read in this story, that adoption was not made legal until it was recorded on the books in 1959. Unintentionally, an attorney had forgotten to file the signed adoption papers. Looking back to what could have come from his mistake, I can only give thanks to God for ruling and overruling that situation.

Beyond this first adoption, I have come to understand that the day I was born again, I was also adopted again. The apostle Paul wrote to believers in Galatia these words: *But when the fullness of the time was come, God sent forth his Son, made of a woman, made under the law, To redeem them that were under the law, that we might receive the adoption of sons* (Galatians 4:4-5 KJV). Other versions say *that we might receive the full rights of sons.* Each of us was physically born as a son of Adam, who sinned and brought separation from God to the entire human race.

However, when we are spiritually born from above, God in His sovereign love makes us His children and places us in His family, giving us all the rights of sons. We are heirs with Christ in the kingdom of God and joint heirs with Him, God's unique Son. What an awesome relationship we have with God the Father, God the Son, the Lord Jesus, and with the Holy Spirit Who brings to us all the presence of God. Children adopted legally become heirs in the family who chose them and can never be disinherited or lose their place in the family. Likewise, the children placed into God's family can never lose their position and have a fixed and certain inheritance.

According to Dr. Charles Ryrie in his Study Bible notes on

the benefits of Christ's death, "In the act of adoption, a child is taken by a man from a family not his own, introduced into a new family, and regarded as a true son with all the privileges and responsibilities that belong to this new relationship... Adoption bestows a new status on the one who receives Christ."

To those who are reading this story, I ask you: "How many times have you experienced birth? And, if you were blessed by being adopted into a loving family, have you experienced adoption into the eternal family of God with all rights and privileges of such a family?" Having the full rights of a daughter in my adopted family did not immerse me in riches, fame, or power. In the family of God, I am blessed with a living hope and an imperishable inheritance kept in heaven, ready to be revealed in the last time, as 1 Peter 1:3-5 states.

We taught our children to sing this little chorus:

> *Happy Birthday to you,*
> *But one will not do.*
> *Take Christ as your Savior,*
> *And then, you'll have two!*

No two adoption stories are alike. What others search for may not be important to your own. Your most important relationship in life is the one you have with a loving Father Who is ready to receive you with all your questions and anxieties. Through receiving His One and Only Son you will come to know a Father who accepts you just as you are, loves you unconditionally, and has already planned your life with a purpose.

APPENDIX ONE

Sister's Day Poem

2009

The following poem was written by Peg and attached to an album of photos of her mother that she brought when she came for a visit. It is a beautiful window into her emotions toward her mother and me.

> *So, to my sister, lately come,*
> *I still have not recovered from*
> *The shock of knowing you exist,*
> *The thought of it still gives a twist*
> *Both to my brain and down my spine*
> *To know that there's a sister mine,*
> *When for so long I'd felt bereft,*
> *Since without siblings I'd been left.*
>
> *I'll never know what Mom was thinking*
> *In keeping all of us from linking.*
> *She knew how much I wanted sibs,*
> *And, yet, she lived this huge-sized fib.*
> *I never would have sat to judge,*
> *My love for her would not have budged.*

I can't imagine how her heart
Was pained when she was forced to part
With her first baby, small and new,
And after just a day or two,
To lay her in another's arms,
To trust that they would keep from harm
This little life, so frail and new,
Then go on living with no view
Of baby's firsts and childhood's joys,
Of books to read and favorite toys,
Of girlhood friends, and teenage trauma,
And all things that make the drama
Of growing up in this old world –
Life's stages for a little girl.

But she chose wisely, well, and true
The parents she provided you.
With God's hand, He brought her luck
And found her Tom and Minnie Brock.
She gave you what she couldn't be –
A mom, a dad, a family.

But, as she left you in their care,
She touched your soul with something rare.
She left you rich in Odom wit,
A happy thing that always fit
Any time and any place
To fill a void or light a face.
This crazy one who gave you birth

Was full of fun and full of mirth!

And since you never knew her heart,
I'm giving you my favorite part
Of what she brought to make life sunny,
And how she was so doggone funny.

In culling through a zillion snaps,
I've tried to portray here, perhaps,
The person you'd have come to know,
Did she not guard her secret so.

Though how she must have hurt inside
To know that when her first born cried,
She couldn't turn your tears to laughter,
And teach you then, forever after,
That God is good, and life is sunny,
And so much of it's always funny.

So she spoiled me with love for two,
Because she couldn't dote on you.
She showered me with time and toys
And things to bring forth kid-like joys.
And through it all, she never knew
Her greatest gift to me was you.

– Peg Owen, 2008

A Photo Album

Mother & Me – 1936

Mother & Me – 1937   Daddy, Mother, & Me – 1938

Mona – 1937

Nita – 5 Years Old

Mother, Daddy, & Nita
Baylor University 1953

Mona & Nita, both in their 40s

Mona & Peg

Mona (in black) & Her Sisters

Nita & Mother – 1985

Mother in her 60s

Daddy, Nita, Ben, & Mother – December 21, 1954

Becky with Ben, Ruth, Ben Jr., Nita with Anna
Christmas – 1962

Ben & Nita – 2013

Nita & Peg – July 2008

Ben & Nita – 50th Anniversary, 2004
Front L-R: Daughters Ruth Welch, Anna Johnson, Ben with Grandson
Cooper Johnson, Nita, Ben's Mother (91), Daughter Rebecca Cook
Back L-R: Granddaughters Casey Welch, Lindsey Johnson, Amber Cook,
Grandson Brian Rogers, Son Ben Rogers Jr., Grandsons Brent Rogers,
Robert Welch Jr., and Stephen Welch

Five Generations – June 2013
Ben's Mother's 100th Birthday

But the mercy of the Lord is from everlasting to everlasting on those who fear Him, And His righteousness to children's children (Psalm 103:17)

About The Author

*N*ita Brock Rogers was adopted at birth and grew up in Shreveport, Louisiana. She earned her B.A. in Biblical Studies from Luther Rice Bible College & Seminary. Nita was secretary for the 1973 Billy Graham St. Louis Crusade, Administrative Assistant to the Director of Evangelism for Florida Baptists, as well as being widely known as a speaker for women's conferences and retreats. She led a women's seminar on prayer and spiritual awakening for the Home Mission Board of the Southern Baptist Convention.

Married for fifty-nine years to Dr. Ben D. Rogers, pastor, evangelist, author and educator, she has served as the administrative assistant of his evangelistic association since 1972. Nita has joined her husband for crusades in England, Korea, Israel, and Africa. She began teaching the Bible at the age of thirteen and currently leads a women's class in her home church. Her current ministry focus is an orphan feeding center in the area of Lilongwe, Malawi. Nita is mother and grandmother of five children, eight grandchildren and eight great-grandchildren.

Connect with Nita

Facebook: https://www.facebook.com/nita.rogers.9
Email: nita.rogers.9@facebook.com